The Singing River

Praise for *The Singing River*

"When Benjamin Morris says of the low country of Mississippi and Louisiana, 'were this landscape a lover / I would leave it without mercy,' we hear the declaration of *amour fou* that binds so many of us to the South. These poems sing the beauty of this captivating, complicated place, a song lush and lyrical until it bursts forth in heat, flood, or other distempered act that may swallow us the way 'the shadow of a barn / eats a black dog whole.' This poet's eye and ear are fine-tuned instruments of perception and attention, well suited to his favored form, the sonnet—the lover's and elegiast's default mode. He also creates an elegant, riverine form to embody the book's remarkable title poem. Let us laud this marvelous debut."

—Brad Richard, author of *Turned Earth*

"The landscapes we inhabit make claims upon us that are often overwhelming in their totality and complexity. And dissecting those claims (of history, of identity, of conflict) but more so, piecing it all back together, is a task uniquely suited for only the most insightful of poets. In *The Singing River*, Benjamin Morris masterfully plumbs the depths of our geo-psychic human capacities, enticing us to question who we are and what we might become. Each poem here reads like a bronze placard to be mulled over for years; each has its own mysterious life energy that's impossible to resist."

—Rodrigo Toscano, author of *The Cut Point* and *The Charm & the Dread*

"At every line's end, Benjamin Morris' *The Singing River* enacts a rare clarity of being. Morris' lyric considers the ways our complex and often contradictory interior lives are nuanced responses to the overwhelming land(s) of the South where 'trees uproot themselves / from the earth to crawl under each other / for shade.' The poems that make *The Singing River* speak the material world of highways, backfiring trucks and our shared ecological life, but faithfully a kind metaphysical logic is being tested too—'the map forgotten the map imagined the map dreamed.' Morris reminds us that the realities we imagine we must also live through and within. Whether by starlight or lantern light *The Singing River* makes legible a South that even in the thicket of its opaqueness is beautiful."

—C.T. Salazar, author of *Headless John the Baptist Hitchhiking*

The Singing River

poems

BENJAMIN MORRIS

Fort Smith, Arkansas

The Singing River

Cover image: Walter Inglis Anderson (1903–1965)
Tern c. 1942, Pen and Ink on Paper
Gift of Mary Pickard in memory of Sandy Ashley
WAMA Permanent Collection

Author photo: Kendra Jones Photography

Edited by Casie Dodd
Design & typography by Belle Point Press

Belle Point Press, LLC
Fort Smith, Arkansas
bellepointpress.com
editor@bellepointpress.com

Find Belle Point Press
on Facebook, Substack,
and Instagram (@bellepointpress)

Printed in the United States of America

29 28 27 26 25 1 2 3 4 5

Library of Congress Control Number: 2025930309

ISBN: 978-1-960215-33-8

SNGR/BPP43

Contents

Heat Wave

In the photo under the headline
the two girls, chin-deep in the lake,
are grinning from one ear to the other,

their faces pressed together so tight
it looks as if one's mouth ends
where the other begins,

a long unbroken chain of milky teeth.
Scarcely eighty degrees in that country,
and they call it a heat wave.

Let me tell you what I know of heat:
I have seen the horizon bend and warp
as though turned in a flash to taffy;

I have seen trees uproot themselves
from the earth to crawl under each other
for shade.

                    Where I call home
you can hear houses sigh and settle
as the glue that binds them melts,

and in the stillness of early evening,
the wind but a distant memory,
the cobwebs cough into flame.

Downtown at noon, the towers
shed all their windows and doors
and bend their spires

to snag the passing clouds—
this, this is what I know of heat.
O frail country,

if this
is where desire has led you,
if this is what you want,

then follow me no further—
for all I have to offer
are the shouts of two grown men

chasing after lightning,
trying to anchor the storm,
as ten miles over

in the next parched parish
the shadow of a barn
eats a black dog whole.

Low Country

All I have ever wanted
is a mountain,
                    a rock
where rivers are born,
on which bracken clusters
and scree falls, where
the map is built,
not splayed: a jagged line
for the eye to grasp onto
in this endless ocean
of sky—

            not these fens
flat as paper from the press,
broken only by canals
and rails signing the fields
in steel. To tower over them
we must only stand up,
to rinse the one tree
from the horizon we need
but squint and it is gone—

            were this landscape a lover
I would leave it without mercy,
no wet letter or backwards glance,
no matter how full its eyes of dew.
It could chase me with storms,
send tornadoes to spin me around,
but still I would shun it
in search of my mind's desire—

the savage join
of crag and cloud,
proof of gravity spurned,
where smoke tendrils north
in the morning and shadows
lie stiff on the slate—where
this far up, this near to the sun,
the only way out is—

Flood Tide

It was because we shunned the upset river
that it brought us what it did: whole trees
shorn of their leaves, strange vessels whose
flags flickered in the breeze, fish which never
learned to swim, their corpses rising bloated
in the sun. The river's gifts were freely given
despite our indifference—that it was riven
by the waters of the melt, the flood floated
downstream as if it were just another barge.
Then it ferried what we could not foresee:
the news, now six months old upstream,
that its denizens had fled. There the large-
print type had run, but here we could not
evacuate. It was summer, and so very hot.

The Names of Storms

Some we speak of as old friends,
reminding us how to prepare
for their arrival—fill the tub

with water, stock the cupboard
with cans. That there are never
enough batteries. Others we recall

as bad neighbors, who left the axe
in the tree, forgot to feed the dog.
Breezing back into town, gone again

just as soon, we can forgive
their itinerance, stopping by just
to check on the roof. But the last

we remember as lovers—
Camille, Andrew, Isabel—
turning our houses upside down,

cutting our power and water
in their fury, leaving our lives
strewn all over the yard,

knowing that in years to come
we will be ravished again
each time we murmur their name.

Returning the Lantern after Ida

Faithful friend,
    companion these last days,
you gave us hope
    once the power had failed
and the night took us
    in its waiting arms.
Reading, eating, bathing
    in this sudden dark,
your glow never wavered,
    only swung gently at our side
as we carried you from room
    to room, as you carried us
through the caverns of our homes.
    When the fury had passed,
you helped us find one another
    in the downed street, helped us
find the scattered pieces
    of ourselves. Rest, now,
hanging on your nail by the door,
    the power restored, the last
of the dusk no longer
    the refuge where we huddled,
wondering what the morning sky
    would reveal, holding
such small and fragile
    starlight in our hands.

Highway 90

Tell me what you know of north and south.
I've never heard of any other road
but me, connecting the brown tannin mouth
of the Pascagoula to the darker wood
of Bois Sauvage to the west. Or so they say.
All I see is water anymore. Water foaming in
forty feet tall, blending the noonday
beach into a filthy gumbo of roof tin,
light pole, drywall, corpses later found
spiked with nails and rebar, and the bridge
over the bay fallen like a matchstick house.
The gifts of latitude: a broken ridge
of the salted bones of the coast's live oaks;
concrete slabs for homes; my compass, smoke.

Gravitron 3000

Praise be to this:
the door clanging shut,
the world outside disappearing,
the night swallowed up
in this new dark.

Glory to the first
tentative spins,
the flight from the ground
as we are lifted
one by one into the air,

and to the swift wind
that whips the breath
from the depths of our lungs.
Pinned against the inner wall,
profess now the prison

of the force that binds us,
our bodies rising as one,
never to be released
save a bolt untighten,
a rivet slip loose,

and the same arms
that hold us
in their invisible embrace
fling us outward
and upward to the stars.

The Making

My mother was bornd between Poplarville an' Picayune an' my father was bornd at Red Church forty mile below New Orleans. . . . My father was a carpenter an' a blacksmith, could make a whole wagon, go out an' cut him a gum tree an' make a whole wooden wagon, an' hubs an' ever'thing. That's how come they didn' take him to de War; leave him at home ter make mule shoes an' things. He was a powerful worker.

—Charlie Bell

Once he had found the one, he stood
back of it a ways and sized up the work:
which way it would fall, what other trees
it would take down as it went, the sound
of branches snapping and roots cracking
like the white-hot flames that powered

his forge. Then, into it: under the power
only of his back and arms, standing
in a pool of sweat, he cracked
his axe into the cut like a fury, the work
showering him with dust and dirt, the sound
a clocklike toll through the trees.

Once down, new light bathing the trees
where it had stood, the making: powered
by the need of its use, the sound
of every tool that he had brought—standing
at attention like soldiers in that war, working
to protect the right of the whip to crack

across his back—filled the air. Cracks,
as the wood split along the grain, the tree
becoming lumber. Whines, as he worked
his blades on the grinding stone, powered

by his foot. Grunts, his oxen standing
and watching him in the heat, the sounds

of lung, muscle, ache and spit, sounds
he barely realized he was making. Cracking
one handle he would fashion another, stand
back to survey his work, lean against a tree
to catch his breath before the power
of necessity drew him back in. The work

yielded pegs for nails, poles for axles, worked
planks and spokes echoed by the sound
of the hammer and adze, the phantom powers
of friction and torque closing up the cracks
in the bed. Overhead, the tips of the trees
whispered in the breeze as dusk filtered into the stand.

Night. The creak of wheels the only sound
as his oxen powered the tree back to the farm,
where he would stand, and park the day's work.

Lepidoptery

Oaken frame, velvet lining, specimens pinned
in even rows. Two boys before the case,
mouthing to each other the names: skinner,
Bowie, butterfly. The lepidoptery of blades.
One palms his hand against the glass, traces
a line from one edge to the next, mimics
the action of the lock—and then erases,
with a quick flip of the wrist, his brother's neck.
Tell me: what man in these woods has not first
been his own son, rapt before the gleaming
rows, sinking into summer as it deepens,
all thoughts of frog and hollow, his fist
swift and fast around the grip, dreaming
of how much, how very much, he will open?

Imagining the Death of My Father on the Pascagoula River

Sometimes I think his truck will backfire,
so that you will be able to hear him
and answer the door. Other times I think
he will come silently, so not to disturb
the catfish in the weedbed, and he will sit
with you a while on the skiff and maybe drop a line
into the water too. He will not catch anything,
because not even Death could coax those old cats up.
I see him living on a houseboat like the others,
evading his taxes and slicing his hands
on the bright scales of his dinner, see him
looking up from checkers to wave at you
on the bayou. He will walk in the woods with you,
hear the wild hog grunting; you will show him
how to break catalpa worms in half,
then thread them inside out so the bream
will smell them sooner. When he returns home
he will tell your mother you still remember how.
He will trim your azaleas in the evening,
then sit in your chair as you practice the trumpet;
he will daub your bloody lips upon his sleeve.
Yes, this is how death must arrive on the river:
like the eyes of the alligator, slipping smooth as shadow
into the summer air, watching, watching the dog.

Highway 57 (to Vancleave)

Don't ask what stories I can tell. To me
your news is an oil slick drying in the sun:
I eat light when the deer pass under
your mother's headlights, spit it out three
hours later when the sirens arrive.
Then it's back to silence: lustrous, clear,
until the moon unveils the shaded air
and the cicadas burn with desire—tonight
desire echoes back, hovering above the black
like fresh mist after rain, off roads named
after children, after whiskey and shame.
So don't come asking down this tarmac—
I took your parents first, for all to see.
Next I'll write your truck onto a tree.

Hospice

how strange
it is
to pack a bag
to stay
in a room
in which neither
the journey
nor the destination
are yours

Sonata in Orange

for Elizabeth Bishop

This morning
I peeled the last clementine,

its brazen skin
falling softly to the floor

as though
it were auditioning for gravity.

I slipped
the fat crescents against my cheek,

letting one sac spray
at a time, the juice running thin

and cold and clear
between my teeth. Early autumn

and I've thrown
the day away to travel:

three o'clock
and through the train window

the sun slides
its knife across my chest;

thick shadows
of house and tomb give way

to fields whose
curves and soft undulations

must have been
what the old painters were looking for,

not what was there
but what we wanted to see—

crops raked
and combed by sunlight, creamy birds

dripping from
the clouds. There's a word in my head

I can't seem
to get out: *panoply*. And another:

vestments. And
another, and another after that, a word

for each
of these folds in the earth, each

of these sheep
salting the plains, words into infinity,

into everywhere,
into all the coughs and rustlings

of all
the other travelers on this train,

into myself,
into nowhere at all. Into the clouds,

placid massive
ice floes sailing the silent sky.

Into colors
not yet seen, into orange, a color

caught between
two lives, spun across the sound

of one belief
forming. No one knew where we were

an hour ago,
gliding to the top of the world

where strange winds
tousled the loose dirt and snow

into a kind of
lunar vegetation, spreading into evening

with a tenderness
received because we could not

ask for it.
Yet there the eye had no house

large enough
anymore to chamber such rich texture.

It seemed too
as though part of the earth

had dropped away
and taken all the color with it,

save for that
we had smuggled with us on the train.

Oh Elizabeth,
you saw sun behind a hill

rim the trees
into blurred and smoky shadows,

you know
the fear of the indistinct

and its awful
and graceful beginnings—where

have you gone,
and why have you left us, alone,

on a train,
avoiding our destination? Night, now,

and the air
empties. They say the cosmos

kills a body
not because of what it does, but because

of what it fails
to do: pressurize the blood, permit the cells

their slow leavings
and unleavings. How swiftly the mind

wraps itself
around this fact, draws near

to the warmth
given off by an idea as violet and

unknowable
as gravity, as the body next to me,

a body reading,
a mind wrapped in the fictions

of its own
fashioning. Beneath us now the waters

roll and swallow
in the moonlight as though made

of molten silver,
in the long languor of things

not having names
nor needing them. Wind stirring the reeds,

a first sound
rippling over the lake, still sounding.

They may not
have bought it but he sure sold it

to them—
the language comes whirling in

on skates,
turning and twisting as if wanting

to recall
a place it had long forgotten,

a place with
clementines and wine, and words

and gestures
ripe for falling into memory's basket,

thatched with stars
whose light still flirts with time.

Soon we will
take down the old patterns from the shelf,

dust them
for the coming evening, retire

to the sunroom
while the birds dream their slim nests

together.
Soon this remembrance too

will be held
to the light like a gem.

We all want
to die near the river: mirror, mirror

on the glass,
enough of the future, tell me my past.

Shore and rock, froth
and foam, tell me where my heart will roam.

Gethsemane

for my daughter

i

One of the first fights we had was whether
they were still boats, when we found
them in the trees. Sails mute of their weather,
oars snapped in the novel tides, sound
of Johnson 18hp motor long silenced,
we said to each other: is this not now a house?
No more did we measure our way in mileage
but rather in slow eddies gained, louse-
eaten food secreted away in attics
where the bloated corpses of the blessed
lay watch over them with rusted axes
and moldspoken dark oaken chests
where their last refuse fermented and flowered.
Blessed? They had found a shaded bower.

ii

Bless us, Father, who found the shaded bower
of Gethsemane, our priest implored as he
celebrated the Mass, a few scant hours
before we heard the floodwalls had breached.
Or so somebody said. I wasn't there—
I was loading rounds into my .38,
praying to my own gods, chance and fair
warning, asking forgiveness were I late
to our assignation. Later I heard
he had drowned at the top of the nave,
kissing the tongue-and-groove cypress boards
of the vessel that carried him to a grave
only his god knew where. How do you bury
a body in a flooded cemetery?

iii

The bodies in the flooded cemeteries
(St Joseph no. 2 and Xavier no. 9)
soon began to float free. At Holy Mary
Our Lady of Sorrow it's said that Compline
was better attended by the dead
than by the living. Dust to dust takes fire,
not water, and so their numbers grew. Help had
not come. Rumors bubbled through the mire
—of helicopters, of Guardsmen, of food—
but each new murmur faded just as swiftly
as the last, and before long we knew
they would not come. There was no cavalry.
Nor was it long before some began to wonder
the sound their words would make, going under.

iv

The sound a word makes as it goes under
a soft wool blanket or past a cracked door
would have come like a jolt of thunder
to our parched ears. As would seeing a floor
to any structure—it had been a year
(is that what they were called? I can never
remember, and my mind is less clear
from having battled the silence, the fever,
and the near-permanent solitude)
and still the waters had not receded,
only teased us with the occasional ruined
husk of roofs and treetops. These we needed
to cling onto just the same—here, alone,
the only shadows cast were our own.

v

The only shadow cast became my own.
It had been weeks (this *was* a word
I knew) since I'd taken the skin and bones
of my castaway and thrown them overboard
after he tried to paddle off without me
as I slept. There are virtues in concealing
weapons in one's shirt, and so I
shot him in the back, and now he'll congeal
with whatever lurks below. Then last night
I heard another shot: a sign of life!
Praise god or gods—or perhaps a suicide,
most everyone now has a tale of a wife
thus gone, a cousin or a lover. Me, well,
all I have is an invented past to sell.

vi

This invented past I have, I'll sell
it to you for a gallon of water. *And what*
would I be doing, risking both my health
and my family's for a story? It's all that
we ever gain, as far as I'm concerned.
What else do you offer? My second child
caught the melt-worm and I've earned
nothing in this goddamn trade except bile
and dice and insomnia. And I this thirst.
What if I spin you a yarn you can then
use to lower anyone's guard while your first
sneaks up and slits their pockets—few men
now keep what they treasure on their vessels.
Better to hold it close to your blood and muscle.

vii

I held it close to my bloody muscle
but still the searing pain would not abate.
Fuck. That at least was a word I could rustle
up from the life before, a word that
you'll never learn. It means *please.* The bastard
went and shot me as I got back on my boat—
All that work weaving loss into a hard
spun cloth and his youngest took my coat
and razored it as I was sewing up the tale;
I'd told him how it was done and he goes
and does it. All that I had left was two bales
of rope, a little food, and wind that wouldn't blow
no matter how hard I swore. That and a soiled
rag around my arm, darkening like oil.

viii

This rag around my arm, grown dark like the oil
paints she used to fling upon the canvas,
is now the flag I fly on the pitch and roil
they sometimes call a sea. Had I an atlas,
I would sail this strapped-together ship
to find her with her easel and her brush
breathing back into the landless landscape
grasses and trees, birds, things we'll never touch
again. But all we have is the self-erasing line
the crest of each wave makes, frothing song
without words save the sideways *I, I, I*
over, over. Whoever used the word was wrong.
This is not a sea, and there is no one
to drown in it, no man, no woman.

ix

Left to drown in it, no man or woman
could forget the floodwaters' acrid kiss
on the skin. It's true—I told the trader one
of the early swimmers began to sizzle and hiss
all over as if she were being fried alive,
and how I tried to wrap her in my shirt
to soothe her, once I had pulled her out of
drowning's way. This was before good clean dirt
had become a currency and could purchase
one's own life in the right market. Anyway,
my shirt stuck to her back and arms and face
and came off only in patches. Since that day
I've not seen her—she vanished that night—
but I pray to my gods for her at first light.

x

I pray to my gods for you at first light.
Your mother and I were separated
from each other on the second night—
the crowd at the depot was a great
wind pulling us this way and that, into
and out of its writhing mass, and a hand
slipped free became a face at a window
locked from the inside. Do you understand?
I never meant to lose you. But that one
moment and you were gone, you with her, still
safe inside her, just weeks away from your own
journey into this troubled ocean. I fill
my cup with you both, and drink deep
each night before I do not sleep.

xi

Each night, because I do not sleep
much anymore, I have taken to naming
the stars anew. We had forgotten them, our need
of gods above us long supplanted by aiming
at the sky to shoot down whatever flew there
and eat it. But even these small gods showed
something to those who were left, that air
rises from water by desire, that nothing known
survives being known. If you must, you can eat
rotten fish-picked bird found floating past.
Forget it had a name; think of it as meat.
I gave you a name, but it didn't last.
I don't remember it now. It's been too long.
The words begin to loosen in the water's song.

xii

The words begin to loosen in the water's song:
what part of me bridges the arm and the head?
It hurts all the time, like it doesn't belong
on my body. My skin is stained beetroot red
but I don't know if that is from the sun
or from the blood of the fish I have caught.
Thank you fish for giving me your thin bones
to write with. My head hurts. I am not
sure like I once was where I am. Are we
near home? Are there still streets below the waves
or have they swum off too? Here, fishy, fishy.
What tender bones you have. What is your name?
A pleasure to meet you. My head, it hurts.
I think I'll make a pillow of this dirt.

xiii

I've never met a bed so soft as dirt.
Sew up the tale. Finish your dinner,
then you can go play. What do I care
for heaven? I was born a sinner
and I'll die one too. I'm sorry I shot you.
No, don't come. You and our daughter
wait here. I'm sorry I forgot you.
What do you mean the floodwalls—the water
can't be stopped? Fishy. Or was it a hard
flat coin? Why would—she was just here—
I left her here and went to make a call.
How could she go and disappear?
A hand slipped free. My eyes hurt. Bury
my heart at Flooded Knee. Will you carry me?

xiv

Will you carry me?
In my fevered dreams,
in this strange alchemy
of mind, what seems
to be your voice
keeps calling out to me—
a light, silvered noise
just like the melody
your mother would hum
as she painted at night.
This I do remember:
one of the last fights
we had was whether
there would be weather.

The Dream of Light

Walter Anderson, Seahorses, ca. 1960

She is born
                    in a sketch,
a curl and a flourish,
a swirl flown off the brush.

The title lies:
                    it is not
ten he is painting but one,
one that grows slowly

as she swims across the page,
swallowing ink like krill—
first her tail,
                    with its ridges

and spines,
                    then her wings,
their textures and bright bone.
By the time she is grown,

dripping with the darkness
of the deep,
                    the ghosts
of her former lives littering

her path,
                    she has woken
into a dream of color,
a flood of golden light

so radiant it draws the shade
near to her in worship,
then dismisses it
                    swiftly away—

asking as she goes
who among us
                    has never wanted
to flare into this world

like a nova,
                    our skin
glowing through the depths of night,
inhaling the soaring dark

to breathe it out again
as the wild and untamable
surface
                    of the sun?

Seven Types of Line

after Walter Anderson

The first line
is the line cast out
over the water,
vanishing at the far point
of the horizon.

The second line
curves in the middle
like a bow, bending
to receive the force
that acts upon it.

The third line
emerges as the first,
travels the same path,
but as it reaches maturity
turns and punctures itself
in the back.

The fourth line
is the line of melody,
borne aloft by a river
of planes—into which
it dives, preys, and surfaces
as a sleek black water bird,
returning with wriggling
in its mouth.

The fifth line
shoots up from the ground
and arcs over the grass

to form a canopy.
On it may be hung
a swing set, a pane of glass,
or a shadow. This line
is not to be trusted.

The sixth line
has not been seen in years.
Its last recorded sighting
observed its ashen pallor
and fraying upon its tail.

The seventh line
curls inward toward
itself—taken between
thumb and forefinger,
it will unfurl as a tongue
unveiling a word:
until it glimpses itself
in a mirror, sees
the shadow of the first line
forming, and so startled,
flees, and disappears.

Highway 29 North (from Ellisville)

Some days, I am almost sorry that they laid
me down: the sunlight caressing the waves
of field grasses, the endless breeze that gives
more of itself with every hour, the late
evening sigh of the treetops as they bend
and stretch to catch the dusk—upland, I rise
and rise into beauty without rest. The sky
above is a bowl that no human hand
can fill—so why, traveler, do you slow to take
its measure? This grass, these silvered lakes
will outlast us all. The psalms along my shoulder
will tell you what the heavens claim to declare—
but here on earth there is no glory other
than the scent of fresh wild lavender in the air.

The Swiftlet

Quickly you shut the door,
grab my arm, lead me out

to the field where the swiftlet
lives—we've been here before,

you and I, hunting mushrooms
or rabbits or something to say,

but today there is sun,
and with it the glint on a wing

too bright to see. Hours pass,
feeling like days. The grass

grows tired of us, stiffens
like a soldier, braving the wind—

and then, just as we are running
out of words, you see it—

and pull me down low, where
it is gone, then there, then gone

again in the tall sheaves,
where, when I tire of you

and stand, the swiftlet was,
where its *was* still is.

Love Song: Carter Mountain

One final turn and here the last light
finds us: a ridge on the western crest,
where long before we met you sought the sight
of your city sleeping, the world below at rest
in the sparkling dark. But tonight you stand
apart, just out of reach, as you search out
some hidden hope, some far talisman
to soothe your troubled heart. The land is mute—
but were there one word, one small *tendresse*
that would restore your smile, your touch,
I would climb this, and then the next,
until the land ran out of hills and all such
silence sank into the sea. Love, we were never
meant for distance. Only nights as long as rivers.

Lies We Tell Tourists

That there is an alley
off Beggar's End where
the wind never blows,

that wisteria here never
blooms on a Tuesday.
We haven't seen a bird

in years, not since
the street war of the '80s,
when they sided with the mice

and the cats ran them all
out of town. That glass
does not shatter, it melts,

that our central library
holds millions of books,
most of them not yet written.

Our river was never a plague pit,
our dump never a parkland—
that our beautiful, beautiful city,

where the *trompe l'œil* oils the mind
sits just inside of fact, but falls
just outside of the eclipse.

Cartocacoethes

after Chris McCabe

Start with the stars.

Log a hundred months
of looking and the heavens

will crack into order:

crabs. Bulls.
Ways home.

Turn next to clouds
and with a shielded eye
read the ice written in the sky:

lattice of daydream
and ship-hope,
scumble
and contour,
distance visible
sought and drunk deep.

See there contrails become
entrails, the pattern
on a rug, the cleft
on a skull, the afterglisten
of rain on a window
key to the fissures
glass conceals.

To begin drawing,
pick any two points

and name the street
you see between them,
and from all those that spiral   outward—

those that end
and those that begin
only where they end—

plot the crises of unbecoming,
the signs that lead you   astray,
followed
into an alley
where someone
marries vomit
to a wall.

Continue on, finding
veins in streets
and streets in leaves,

the one in two
and the two in
the stars,

pockmarked in the night—

mark your legend
with crosses and buttons,
zippers, clasps,

the need
to loosen bodies carved
out of each other,
limbs leading to extremity
where dwells
the darkness of the end
of the map,

vessels
falling off
the page,

dragons, chimaeras,

then the body regained:

one sprawl askew,
the other akimbo,
each a map of the other,

every curve and fold stained through
with the ink that skin brings:

scrawl of nail on
edge of hip on
slur of flesh on
logic of bone.

Dare yourself to stop:
sirens a map to the crime,
steam a map to the ground,
salt a map to the sea,
smoke to fire, shards to mirror,
shoppers to the store—

what flees from us
a map to the self,
to the center
of the word,
cartocacoethes
in the end
a map
to madness:

the map to   the map past   the map sketched   the map lost

the map of   the map fixed   the map smudged   the map forgotten

the map from   the map faded   the map scattered   the map imagined

the map around   the map torn   the map erased   the map dreamed.

And when the drawing is done—
the brush rinsed, the palette scraped—
here is what you will have made:
a map to the face through the voice,

a map to the tongue through the pulse,
the nerve, the cortex, the seahorse,
the day, the place, and the hour
you first made love under the stars,

those same nightless and cloudless eyes
watching us eons ago—a flake of obsidian
scratched in the night, map to our father,
sculpting our past in a cave.

Old Highway 80 East (to Meridian)

With luck, you'll never see me again.
Diverted not once but twice—first from your day
then again from the route you planned to take
you reach for the map, as if my thin
black ribbon could be unwound. But no.
Unlike my younger brother, who drapes across
this state like a belt, all I own is loss:
my length, cut like a root when the hoe
bites down; my woods, cleared for either concrete
or graves; even my one last town is named
Lost Gap. Behold its cabin hollowed by flame
and be grateful, friend, that as soon as we meet
we depart. But ask yourself before you go:
you don't really believe in luck—do you?

Making a Midden

First the slice into the tousled sand,
the kick and twist to open the ground's grin.

October looms overhead, stitches the earth
with leaves, whispers to us of our worth.

But this pit must be dug, its litter dispensed—
this twice-crushed mug, this wine-stem rinsed

in grit, this ceramic cracked into an edge.
The shovel tamps the dirt, smooths it to a fresh

new sheet: this house collapsed, this street a ruin,
this city known only as a map of the forgotten,

let the nosy trowels come—and in this midden
find not what was sought but what was given,

blackened glass, a split pill bottle in which to carry
the distant death-rattle of the gods we buried.

Highway 14 East (from Louisville)

Normally they skip and jump like a child,
leap from car to car, pick one up here
and set it down again there, bathed in air
and dripping in glass and light. The fields
a mosaic of loss, a maze of downed pines,
crushed trucks, and wires hissing rivers
of sparks.
                    Old news. *Passé*. What will never
be forgotten is this: the thin, distant whine
before the roar, the sky first black then green,
the shadow passing over me to a house
where it sucked the shoes and socks off their feet,
then took the youngest up by the knees.
Her mother held her by the hair until it passed—
and there was nothing, nothing that it would mean.

Parasailing: Pensacola Bay

The boat speeds up: clouds gather overhead.
Strapped in under the chute, inch by inch
we're lifted into the sky, the winch
unspooling us as from a coil of thread—
from here the coast unfolds before our eyes,
where countless miles of dune and sand
extend below, the sea and the land
holding each other in an endless embrace.
The hour slips into the wind. Lowered down,
the water's surface darkens to a slate
on which the skiff veers east, writes
its name in frothing ink upon the sound.
To the west the storm has swallowed the day;
as we alight, we stand upon the bay.

The Fact of the Coast

. . . after all this time, what has the beach left to say to the tide?

—Andrew Philip

Already the town has melted into the fog:
a moment ago and we were lost in a thicket

of walls wrought in glass and steel,
bound in paints whose names would swallow

the tongue. Then caravans speckling the green,
clusters of plastics tapering away, then—

nothing. No brick, no cable nor girder nor car,
just the train flowing forward with the wind,

the hills on our left, the sea on our right
as far as we can see. There is nothing land loves

so much as ending: the edges of the cliffs
leap out over the waves, are bathed in spray

and sun-flecked sealight, as the thin gullies
inland rush downhill to meet them. Even

the long arc of the train seems designed
to bring us as close as possible to the brink,

clasping the last meters of sandstone and turf
where the gorse blossoms buffet our eyes—

so sometimes I think we must have dreamt it,
this stone cottage that slides into view on the shore,

cradled in the blood-tinted rock, its ceiling
collapsed, windows vacated, its one room sheltering

the winds alone, its floor flung wide to the sky.
Overhead the gulls circle but refuse to land,

their shadows rippling on the dark wet moss.
And then it is gone—slipping back under a cliff

just as soon as we have seen it, too soon to know
if it was a house or a fort, Our Lady of the End

of the Island, Holy Sepulcher of Shale.
The train veers back toward the earth,

our bottles slowly draining like the day.
Soon we will pass the Law but will not see it:

for the fact of the coast has left us deckled
with the truth, that somewhere beneath us

is a border where one country bleeds
into the next, and somewhere inside us

is another—a border between the lid
and the eye, the breath and the lung,

the pull toward elegy and the need
to pelt the page with rocks until it breaks.

Tonight

They should have made it a verb: *to*
night: to reach for a body;

alt., to come to the end of wandering,
to find harbor. So tonight we lay

coiled against each other, the breeze
grazing our skin after an evening

dimming swiftly through the window.
Had we lost this word for the hour outside,

would we still speak of it as a forest
yet to be charted, with your eye trailing

mine, the sound of your body changing shape
in the dark, dragging the shadows with it?

In the warmth my thoughts give way to water,
this room
composing itself anew

for you to wake into it—moonlight
etched on the mantel and the chairs

affixed to the wall, the bed
on the ceiling, rolling in the lap and tide of the sheets—

and were there no angels waiting
to save us from the storm, we would stay here

all night, praying, *deliver us to evil,*
for ours is the wreckage,
                                        the body,
                                                  the cry.

The Singing River

According to legend, after the Pascagoula Native American tribe of southern Mississippi lost a battle against their enemies, the Biloxi, rather than face massacre the remaining members of the tribe joined hands and sang in unison as they walked into the river that now bears their name.

These are the things
I know to be true:

when boys go off to war
they come back two feet taller

or in a box.

Virgin pine, six feet
in length,
even if
their bodies were elided
in an ecstasy of heat and light.

This too I know is true:
that pine forests
echo with the memory
of the not-yet-dead,

that the stand
in the upper Pascagoula
quivers with the names

that inhabit our newspapers,
pages that ink
our dead
onto their own.

What else I know

is that Brett Patterson,
named Pat, Patty,
or Dickhead—
not like Josh Cook,
who was always just Chode
until he went off to war
and then
came home again—

both Brett and Josh
were born
sons of the river,

crashing through the brush,
wading to the shore
where sand tickles the soles
of the feet
and the *scritch-scritch*
of fiddler crabs
forms a kind of lullaby.

The voices of the river
ghost over the dawn:

sleep on our bank
dredge up your dreams—

we have been waiting
years for you
to come hear us,

this choir assembled
beneath the murky surface,

where roots suck the soil

for color to spurt forth

like the carotid shredded by shrapnel—

listen
listen again to the song
the dead sing
on being lifted
from the earth—

and are there words, Pat,
is there any scant
or furtive praise

for the men who would say
to you *leave*
this place, *go*
to the desert,
where the wind strips the sense
from your body like sweat?

Here on the rope swing
sworn to the laws of gravity
the blood wakens,
is woven into the breath
of the wind
and the splash
of the fall,

the young cells
pleading
let us grow, let us flower
like the trees in the wood,
like the sun on the skin,

let our days and our divisions
not be curtaïled by an order
given, a position taken.

The marrow breathes deep
in its casing,
dark weavings of protein,
laughter, and names for cunt—

Patty, you who would taste
the inside of a body
long before any of us

in a pine cabin
your grandfather built
on the riverbend,

you who
jammed your fingers inside
her, searching for a hollow
to be sounded
even as
she bit her tongue to blood—

now you taste only
her memory, alone
in the desert, thumb
bracing the stock, index locked
on the trigger
dreaming
of the writhing
she wrought upon it.

Will you fire? Will
you—
or will there be
nothing to wake to
in the morning,

nothing to name or taste,
your brains blotting the flag like stars?

The voices will continue to echo
long after the recollections
are rinsed clean

of your helmet:
the gist of that night,
waking at dawn
on a pine floor.

Can you hear them now,
can you make out
the words?

The river cannot leave the land
without giving itself
up too,

can no more forget the land
than the land forget
the dead it has reclaimed—

the dreamers,
the liars and lovers—

Patty, did you think
that what you called
her *honeypot*

was just a token,
admission to the rites
of men,
men whose desires
crouch behind
a mudbrick wall,

sun raining down upon the roof,
their shouts a torrent
of loss to come, their rifles

extended, their rifles become their face?

Did you think
that what you left behind
on the river,
wrapped
in a blanket of sweat
could ever escape naming?

That was the same year
we rowed far up the river basin,
docked at Pine Island,
our fathers' .22s
on our backs, oiled
and primed
for practice—

shooting at cans, bottles, rotten
fruit, anything that would
shatter when asked,

Chode too
at the wing,
our lookout
swearing

at each sharp report
like his life depended on it,

deep in the wood
where the glass shrapneling
the leaves

became a kind of melody,
each shard softly glinting
with the question
whose answer eludes
even you:

When did you know?
when did you enlist,
decide *today*

is the day the forest collapses
into sand—sand in which

to write the names of the dead,
sand that has no river
to wash them away,

sand in which
you take your finger

and trace your own.

Patty, will you too
come back
from the desert to the forest
with the knowledge
no tree harbors:

that we do not
come home
to sing
as the waters swallow us,

we come home
in a pine coffin
draped in a flag
of stolen years,

that we are only here
in this broken dark
of sand, rope, blood, and cunt
until we are lifted,
are borne clean away?

Brett. Pat. Patty. Dickhead.
My brother, my song,
agent of the dusk,

until you return
your name will never
be worn as it was
on the river,

where you left it on the bank
to dry—

your name now just *Patterson*,
stitched on your uniform

like a cloth prayer
murmured over and over:

I am still alive
I am still alive
I am still

Notes

The epigraph of "The Making" comes from an oral history with Charlie Bell, a former slave from Poplarville, MS, who was freed at nine years old when the Civil War ended. Bell's account is recorded in *Mississippi: A Documentary History*, edited by Bradley G. Bond (UPM, 2005).

"Seven Types of Line": Walter Anderson drew his ideas about basic elemental forms from Adolfo Best-Maugard's book *A Method of Creative Design*, before adapting them to his own ends.

The title of "Lies We Tell Tourists" comes from a now-defunct column that ran for several years in the *Guardian* newspaper; it is much missed.

"The Fact of the Coast" was written for the 50 Counties project in England in 2009, representing Northumberland, on the border with Scotland. Here the word "caravan" is the British term for mobile home or RV, and "the Law" is a large hill outside the Scottish village of North Berwick.

Special thanks to the family of Walter Inglis Anderson (1903–1965), who graciously allowed the use of his *Tern* sketch for the cover—a dream come true.

Much of this work was written under the provision of two Literary Arts Fellowships from the Mississippi Arts Commission in 2010 and 2018, for which I remain grateful. Thanks as well to Aimee Nezhukumatathil for selecting "The Dream of Light" as the winner of the 2021 Words and Music Competition for Poetry. To those who played unique roles in the shaping of this book—Sara Hudson, Hannah Star Rogers, Ryan Van Winkle, Helen Mort, Clare Harmon, and Benjamin Aleshire—thank you. Most of all, I am grateful to my family, who never once asked *why*.

Acknowledgments

My thanks to the editors of the publications in which these poems first appeared, at times in slightly earlier versions:

Amerarcana: The Bird and Beckett Review: "Cartocacoethes," "The Fact of the Coast"
The Dark Mountain Journal: "Low Country"
Deep South: "Returning the Lantern after Ida"
field: a journal of ecology: "Highway 90"
The Man Who Ate His Book: The Best of Ducts, Vol. II: "Imagining the Death of My Father on the Pascagoula River"
The Independent on Sunday (UK): "Heat Wave"
The Island Review: "Gethsemane"
Leaf Litter: "Flood Tide"
Louisiana Literature: A Review of Literature and the Humanities: "The Making"
Making Sense: For An Effective Aesthetics: "The Names of Storms"
Mid/South Sonnets: A Belle Point Press Anthology: "Old Highway 80 East (to Meridian)"
Mississippi Aesthetic: "The Swiftlet"
The May Anthologies: "Tonight," "Sonata in Orange," "The Singing River"
The Peauxdunque Review: "Lepidoptery," "Seven Types of Line," "The Dream of Light"
The Poetry Buffet Anthology / New Orleans Poetry Journal Press: "Lies We Tell Tourists"
Salvation South: "Highway 57," "Love Song: Carter Mountain"
Stirring: "Highway 14 East"
The Southern Review: "Gravitron 3000"
Susurrus: "Making a Midden"

About the Cover Art

Walter Inglis Anderson (1903–1965)
Tern c. 1942, Pen and Ink on Paper
Gift of Mary Pickard in memory of Sandy Ashley
WAMA Permanent Collection

From the Walter Anderson Museum of Art:

Tern is a perfect example of Walter Anderson's mastery of line. The artist has drawn this striking image in ink with absolutely no hesitation in his hand. Anderson's knowledge of form and use of negative space is put on display beautifully in this work as he uses minimal lines to create the piece. With a few strokes of his pen he has composed not just the image of a bird but an expression of all that the bird symbolizes—flight, freedom, peace, perseverance.

A native of Mississippi, Benjamin Morris is the author of *Coronary* (Fitzgerald Letterpress, 2011), *Hattiesburg, Mississippi: A History of the Hub City* (Arcadia/History Press, 2014), and *Ecotone* (Antenna, 2017). He holds an MSc in English literature and creative writing from the University of Edinburgh, and among other honors has received a Pushcart nomination, the Academy of American Poets Prize from Duke University, and the Chancellor's Medal for Poetry from the University of Cambridge, where he earned his PHD. The recipient of academic and creative fellowships from the Mississippi Arts Commission and Tulane University, his writing appears regularly in the United States and Europe. He lives in New Orleans.

Belle Point Press is a literary small press
along the Arkansas-Oklahoma border.
Our mission is simple: Stick around and read.
Learn more at **bellepointpress.com**.